Road Makers and Breakers

and Breakers

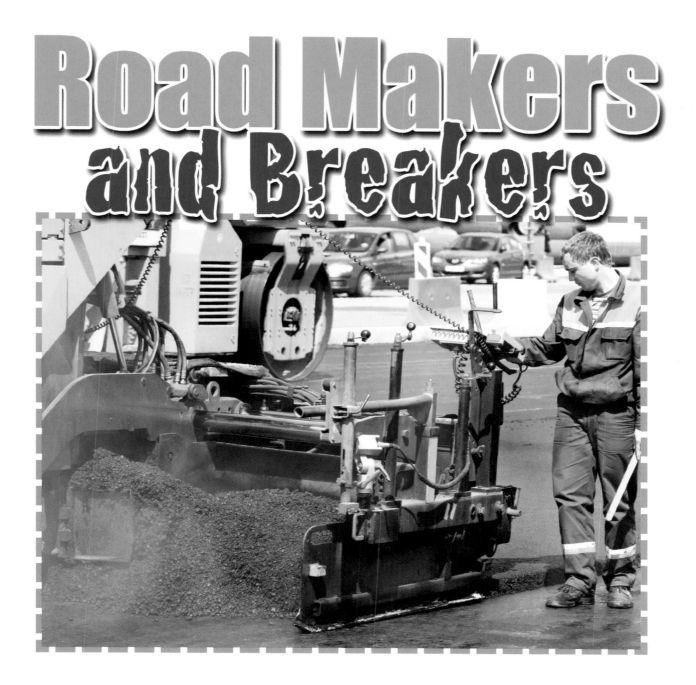

Lynn Peppas

🌲 **Crabtree Publishing Company**

www.crabtreebooks.com

Created by Bobbie Kalman

Author
Lynn Peppas

**Publishing plan research
and development**
Sean Charlebois, Reagan Miller
Crabtree Publishing Company

Editorial director
Kathy Middleton

Editor
Molly Aloian

Proofreader
Crystal Sikkens

Photo research
Samara Parent

Design
Samara Parent

**Production coordinator
and prepress technician**
Samara Parent

Print coordinator
Katherine Berti

Photographs
Keystone Press: © Pittsburgh Post-Gazette/Zumapress:
    pages 30, 31
Shutterstock.com: front cover, title page, pages 4, 6 (top),
    7, 8, 9, 10, 12-13, 14, 16, 17, 18, 20, 24, 25 (top), 26, 27 (both),
    28, 29 (both); Feliks Gurevich: page 11; Thomas Riggins:
    page 15
Thinkstock.com: back cover, pages 3, 5, 6 (bottom), 19, 21,
    22, 23
Wikimedia Commons: Imprezzive1: page 25 (bottom)

Library and Archives Canada Cataloguing in Publication

Peppas, Lynn
    Road makers and breakers / Lynn Peppas.

(Vehicles on the move)
Includes index.
Issued also in electronic format.
ISBN 978-0-7787-3020-0 (bound).--ISBN 978-0-7787-3025-5 (pbk.)

    1. Road machinery--Juvenile literature. 2. Earthmoving
machinery--Juvenile literature. I. Title. II. Series: Vehicles on
the move

TE223.P46 2012   j629.225   C2012-900888-5

Library of Congress Cataloging-in-Publication Data

Peppas, Lynn.
    Road makers and breakers / Lynn Peppas.
       p. cm. -- (Vehicles on the move)
    Audience: 5-8
    Includes index.
    ISBN 978-0-7787-3020-0 (reinforced lib. bdg. : alk. paper) --
    ISBN 978-0-7787-3025-5 (pbk. : alk. paper) -- ISBN 978-1-4271-7944-9
    (electronic PDF) -- ISBN 978-1-4271-8059-9 (electronic HTML)
    1. Earthmoving machinery--Juvenile literature. 2. Excavating
    machinery--Juvenile literature. I. Title.

TA725.P47 2012
621.8'65--dc23
                                                    2012004057

Crabtree Publishing Company
www.crabtreebooks.com   1-800-387-7650

Printed in Canada/042012/KR20120316

**Published in Canada
Crabtree Publishing**
616 Welland Ave.
St. Catharines, Ontario
L2M 5V6

**Published in the United States
Crabtree Publishing**
PMB 59051
350 Fifth Avenue, 59th Floor
New York, New York 10118

**Published in the United Kingdom
Crabtree Publishing**
Maritime House
Basin Road North, Hove
BN41 1WR

**Published in Australia
Crabtree Publishing**
3 Charles Street
Coburg North
VIC 3058

Contents

Road-building Vehicles

A vehicle is a machine that moves people and things from one place to another. Some vehicles also do work. Many vehicles, such as cars, trucks, and buses, travel on roads, streets, and highways. Road-building vehicles are needed to make the streets and highways that other vehicles travel on.

We can travel long distances on streets and highways thanks to road-building vehicles.

Many different vehicles are needed to build a road. Each does a different job. Some road-building vehicles break up the ground to make pathways for new roads or to repair old roads. Other vehicles turn the pathways into new roads that are ready to travel on.

These road-building vehicles are making a highway bigger.

Excavators

There are roads everywhere! Sometimes trees and hills must be cleared to make new roads. An excavator is a big vehicle that breaks up the ground and gets the land ready for a road. It moves on crawler tracks instead of wheels. Crawler tracks help the excavator move on all kinds of **surfaces** without getting stuck.

Crawler tracks are steel plates that are joined together.

Special attachments can be added to excavators for different jobs. This claw helps the excavator pull out tree trunks.

An excavator is great at digging. It has a long arm or boom in the front. The arm is attached to a rotating platform called the house. This is where the driver sits. There is a large bucket on the end of the arm. The bucket has long teeth that are used for digging.

Backhoe Loaders

A backhoe loader is a vehicle that can do more than one job. The front of the vehicle has a large, wide bucket for picking up rocks and dirt. On the back of the vehicle there is a backhoe, or shovel, that is used for digging.

A backhoe loader moves on four tires with deep **treads**. It moves easily and quickly around a worksite. Backhoe loaders dig up and move dirt and rocks. They also help flatten the ground for a new road.

Mobile Cranes

A mobile crane is a vehicle that lifts and moves heavy objects. To be mobile means to be able to move from place to place. A mobile crane is sometimes called a truck crane because the crane is part of a truck. A mobile crane drives to a jobsite on roads.

telescopic arm

*A mobile crane has a **telescopic** arm that can be extended to reach high places.*

Mobile cranes have special feet called outriggers. The outriggers stop them from falling over when they lift heavy things. Mobile cranes move steel bars to build roads called **overpasses**. They also move large pipes to build **drains** at the sides of a road.

outriggers

Bulldozers

Bulldozers are tough vehicles. They move on crawler tracks instead of wheels. The steel tracks have deep metal **ridges** that grip the ground and help them climb up or down hills without sliding. Bulldozer tracks also help to level or flatten the land.

blade

A bulldozer has a steel blade that pushes heavy dirt in the front. Some bulldozers have a ripper, or claw, in the back. The ripper tears up hard ground or old roads.

Bulldozers rip up old roads and push and flatten out bumpy surfaces.

ripper

Dump Trucks

A dump truck carries heavy loads from one place to another. Some dump trucks can carry loads that are over 30 tons (27 metric tons). The back of the dump truck has an open box called a bed. Vehicles such as excavators fill the bed with dirt or rocks.

This excavator is loading sand into a dump truck.

Dump truck beds have doors that open at the very back. Arms called lifts push the bed up at the front. The load drops out through the open back.

*Dump trucks are used to load **asphalt** into road-building machines called pavers.*

Milling Machines

Old roads are sometimes torn up so new ones can be made. An asphalt milling machine is a vehicle that tears up old roads. It moves slowly on crawler tracks. A milling machine pushes a large wheel in front called a cutter drum. The drum has sharp steel teeth that rip a road into pieces.

Milling machines tear up asphalt that can later be recycled and used again on other roads.

conveyor belt

The small pieces of asphalt are moved up a **conveyor belt**. The conveyor belt looks like a long neck that comes out of the front of the milling machine. The pieces of asphalt fall off the belt and into a dump truck that drives ahead of the milling machine.

cutter drum

Soil Compactors

A soil compactor is a vehicle that rolls over bumpy ground. A large, heavy drum in front packs down the dirt to make it hard and smooth. The drum has metal bumps on it that are flat on top. These push the dirt down even more.

Some soil compactors also push a blade, which is attached to the front of the vehicle. The blade spreads loose dirt. Other soil compactors have large wheels in the back with deep treads. Some have another drum on the back with flat, metal bumps that pushes the soil down, too.

A blade on the front of a soil compactor helps to level out the dirt before it's compacted.

Scrapers

A scraper is a vehicle that scrapes the top of the ground. It helps make the ground level or flat. Scraping away layers of dirt is a hard job. Sometimes powerful tractors or bulldozers have to help scrapers move forward.

A scraper pulls one or more large blades that cut into the ground. The blades scrape off the top layer of soil and collect it into a scraper bowl behind the blade. When the bowl is full, the scraper empties the soil out and begins scraping again.

bowl

To empty the scraper's bowl, the front wall is raised and then the back panel of the bowl moves forward and pushes the dirt out the front.

Road Graders

A road grader is used after a scraper to finish flattening out a road. A grader pushes a long, steel blade to smooth over small bumps or loose soil on the surface of a road. The blade is in the middle of the vehicle. Some graders have another blade attached to the front of the vehicle.

A road grader is sometimes called a blade.

A road grader is similar to a scraper, but instead of collecting the dirt, a grader just pushes it. It pushes dirt toward the back and off to the sides of the vehicle. Graders can also make a small slope in a road so that rain will run off to the sides instead of collecting in the middle of the road.

Graders are used to prepare a road for asphalt.

Concrete mixers

Concrete mixers are trucks that are used to make concrete. Concrete is made by mixing cement, sand or gravel, and water together. Concrete mixers have a large drum that turns to keep the concrete from hardening before it is ready to be used.

Concrete mixers are used to make overpasses.

Some roads need a street gutter or curb. A street gutter is a lower area on either side of a road. Rain water runs off the road and into the gutter. Some gutters have a curb. A curb is a concrete border at the edge of a street. Concrete mixers are used to make curbs and gutters.

Sometimes concrete mixers pour concrete into curbing machines to make curbs.

Pavers

A paver is a vehicle that lays asphalt on the ground to make a road. The asphalt is mixed with sand and crushed stones. A paver moves very slowly. It only moves about 100 feet (31 meters) per minute.

This dump truck is loading a paver with asphalt.

There is a big open box called a hopper on the front of a paver. A dump truck fills the hopper with asphalt. The paver heats the asphalt until it is black and runny. A spreader called a screed is at the back of the paver. It spreads the asphalt evenly and makes it the right thickness.

Pavers repair old roads and make new roads.

27

Road Rollers

Road rollers are vehicles that flatten out dirt or asphalt roads. They are very heavy machines that move on large, smooth drums. Some road rollers have one drum, and others have up to three. Each drum weighs over six tons (five metric tons).

Some road rollers have drums that can be filled with water to make them heavy. When they are emptied, these rollers are easy to move from place to place. Other road rollers are sprayed with cool water as they roll over hot asphalt. This stops the asphalt from sticking to the drum.

This road roller's drum was sprayed with water to keep it from sticking to the asphalt.

Some road rollers, like this one, vibrate, or move quickly back and forth. This flattens and smoothes the asphalt even more.

Line Painters

Line painters are vehicles that paint lines on a road. Drivers must stay between the lines when on the road. A line painter moves slowly at about 10 miles per hour (16 km/h). Sometimes trucks with flashing arrows follow line painting trucks so an accident does not happen.

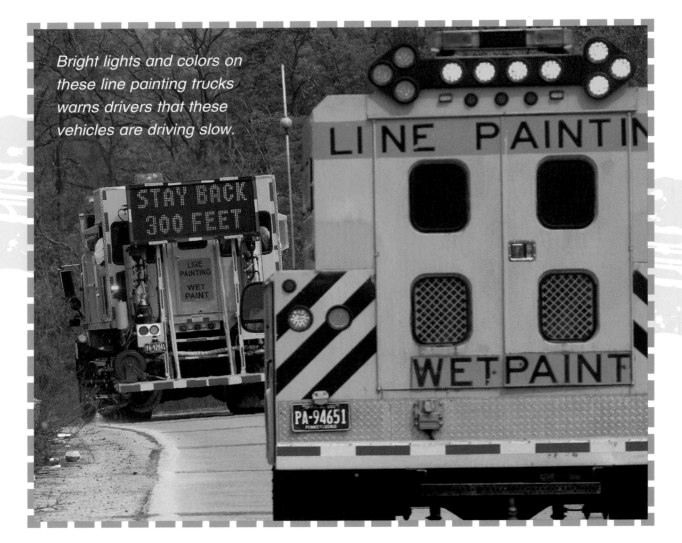

Bright lights and colors on these line painting trucks warns drivers that these vehicles are driving slow.

Line painters have **nozzles** that stick out from the sides of the truck. Paint sprays out of the nozzles onto the road. The paint is sometimes mixed with little glass beads. This makes the paint shinier so drivers can see the lines better.

This line painting truck is painting yellow lines. The truck also carries white paint because some lines need to be white.

Glossary

asphalt A mix of materials used to pave roads

conveyor belt A round strip of material that moves constantly around two wheels on either end. The strip carries objects from one end to the other.

drain An area where water flows and empties into

nozzle A small hose or pipe

overpass A road that is built over another road so that traffic is not stopped

ridge A raised bar or hill

surface The top part or layer

telescopic Something that has parts that fit one inside the other

tread The raised areas of a tire

Index